The Strength of Being Tender

Love Is Like a Butterfly

Dr. James E. McReynolds

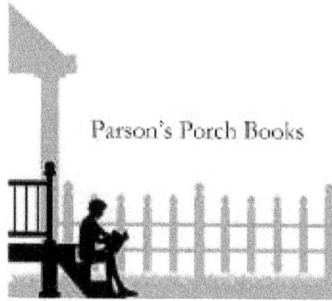

Parson's Porch Books

The Strength of Being Tender
ISBN: Softcover 978-1-960326-02-7
Copyright © 2022 by James E. McReynolds

Parson's Porch Books is an imprint of Parson's Porch *&* Company (PP*&*C) in Cleveland, Tennessee. PP*&*C is a self-funded charity which earns money by publishing books of noted authors, representing all genres. Its face and voice is **David Russell Tullock** (dtullock@parsonsporch.com).

Parson's Porch *&* Company *turns books into bread & milk* by sharing its profits with the poor.

www.parsonsporch.com

The Strength of Being Tender

Contents

Dedication

To Ethan Coffin, my grandson, a sophomore
at Lafayette College, the most loving
and gentle young man I have ever known.

Foreword

Gentleness is infectious. I could feel the thought of it affecting my very mood and spirit as I read the early, unpublished pages of this book for the first time.

We live in a warring, contentious world where most people think they must struggle to survive. Sometimes it does seem to be that kind of world, with people always choosing sides and arguing with others about what we should think and how we should behave. This is a particularly fractious time in our national history, when everybody seems to feel that he or she must enlist in this or that cause and oppose certain ideas or ways of thinking that others are expressing so forcibly.

I have felt it, and so have you.

But as I read Jim's book it began to assure me that life doesn't have to be that way. There is a gentle way—a loving way—that beckons us to a completely different kind of being and thinking. The people of the world don't have to be at odds with one another. We don't have to take sides and contribute to the tension and ugliness.

I like Jim's letters from God in this book—the way he imagines the Supreme Being communicating with him to reassure him about living the beautiful, gentle life he describes in various chapters of the book. I don't believe we often think about the divine gentleness. We're most more likely to remember a strong, demanding figure like the one so often depicted in the pages of the Old Testament. Yes, the gentleness is there too.

I also like that Jim begins his book by talking about butterflies. What could be daintier or more gentle than a butterfly? I often enjoy seeing one—preferably the big yellow butterflies that are easy to see as they flit softly and gently from one place to another in our yard—and imagining what their souls must be like, if they have souls. They make life and beauty so effortless.

Thinking of this, I remember a special occurrence in my life, many years ago. My wife and two sons and I were traveling across the country and had stopped somewhere in the mountains of Colorado. We had trekked off-road into some quiet and lonely meadow high in the crags of that beautiful state, where we came upon a field full of yellow flowers. As far as the eye could see, there were hundreds and hundreds of butterflies— probably thousands of them—flying from place to place on those flowers.

It was like an incredible paradise. I was several yards ahead of my wife and boys. I was so totally entranced by this magical scene that I had to stop, remove all my clothes, and literally dance my way through the meadow.

Our little son Kris, who must have been eight or ten years old at the time, was the first to come up from the tree line into the meadow and see his dad.

"Mom, hurry!" I heard him yell. "Come here fast! Dad's gone crazy!"

I hope that if I were to come upon a similar scene today, so many years later, that I would react in a similar way. I believe I would, just thinking about it. I could not cavort as gracefully now, given my considerable age, but I'm sure that my sense of being in paradise would be as overwhelming today as it was then. I would have to know what a terrifically special and heavenly situation it was.

I know we forget that the world can be like that meadow if we only suspend our usual ways of regarding it and the gentleness and tenderness as well as the harder, more difficult aspects of daily living.

Jim's excellent book, like several other books he has written, will remind us of the whole picture and help us see things in a proper perspective.

Thanks Jim.

John R. Killinger
Warrenton, Virginia

Gentleness in the Butterfly

After my brother David died more than four years ago, I shared the story of asking God for a confirmation that David was now filled with the joy of heaven. A few days later, as I walked back home from church, a yellow and black butterfly landed on my shoe. It stayed there for several minutes.

Yellow butterflies are said to be a sign of joy. Seeing one means a contact with the gentleness of God's presence. If one lands on you, this is an indicator of departed souls who are filled with joy and peace and endless love.

When I was called as pastor for Pilgrim Presbyterian Church in Cameron, Missouri in the early '70s, I was inspired by Dolly Paton's song, "Love is like a butterfly, a rare and gentle thing." (James E. McReynolds, *Joy Comes in the Mourning: Love Is Forever*, pp. 17-19)

Since childhood the beauty of butterflies fascinated me. As I grew older, I found that butterflies symbolize eternal life. Every time I see a butterfly, I think of the people I have loved who have departed. Their memories will never die.

Gentle butterflies have a purpose in our lives. Often when conducting a funeral, a butterfly lights on the casket. Butterflies appear for those who are left behind. When talking with one of the beloved women in my congregation about how my preaching had affected her life. A yellow and black butterfly landed on my shoulder. She told me that I was like a butterfly. "You have come into my life like a delicate butterfly," she said.

I became overjoyed at the thought that I could brighten somebody's life like God and others have brightened mine.

Butterflies are fragile. They cannot survive without external heat provided by the sun. The heat fuels the muscles used to fly with their wings. In cloudy conditions, butterflies are like a solar-powered aircraft, is helpless. We do not spot any butterflies in early morning hours. That is one reason they use their energy to fly off to warmer places such as Mexico or the Caribbean.

Butterflies are a delicate reminder of beauty. What joy to witness one of them in flight. We appreciate the transformation they undergo before becoming winged beauties. Metamorphosis is the name for the process which lasts about a month. That transformation inspires us. Some species live for only a few days. No adult butterfly lives more than one year. Regardless of the brief life span, butterflies enjoy the moments they have on earth.

Nothing in a caterpillar tells us it is going to become a butterfly. It's a miracle. The wonder is like confetti from God celebrating love. A woman living in Ukraine was on the news. She gently held a beautiful butterfly. When the war with Russia is over, a butterfly will still be beautiful.

When a butterfly flies toward a bridge, it shies away from the dark shadows underneath. They take the long way around.

Rain and wind compound the problems started by a layer of clouds. Older butterflies quickly become battered and become easy prey for predators. In places like Nebraska, there is a lot of times of drought and uncomfortable heat. That's when we see many butterflies. In the winter and during the wet and windy weather, severe depletion of the population takes place with recovery taking years.

Butterflies teach us how to ease our way through changes. Perhaps, I am a mystic. Something new and joyful appears to unfold when I spot a butterfly. I believe I fly gracefully above barriers that attempt to hold me back. The butterfly spirit restores lightness in us. I embrace unbridled joy. Early Christians believed the butterfly represented our soul on the journey.

Butterflies make us sensitive to the nectar and aroma of living in the moment. Our inner butterfly emerges from its purpose when the timing is perfect. Christian theology could use a metaphor for Christology as stages of divinity. The caterpillar is a being of this world. The chrysalis is the tomb. The butterfly is the resurrection.

Throughout world history butterflies have been considered sacred. The monarch dates back more than 300 million years ago. Their migrations began long ago. Some students who majored in biology tell me that once impregnated, the females lay nearly 500 eggs the size of the head of a pin on the back of a leaf. The butterfly feeds on the asclepias plant for a couple of weeks. The caterpillar hangs from a branch of the leaf. They weave a bright green silk net around its body. It becomes the chrysalis where it becomes a butterfly. As it breaks through the chrysalis, the form and colors can be distinguished. Its wings dry and harden. This miracle lasts about six weeks.

My fascination with butterflies sparks my spiritual journey. Two young women in my family have taken biology classes that go deep. Unlike the biological classes at Carson-Newman University, where the best we could do was to dissect an ugly earthworm.

The butterfly's color protects it in winter. They alight on tree trunks by the millions. They fold their wings to show their undersides and blend their colors into a tree's bark.

I offer this look at the biology, the life, and stories of butterflies during this time of transformation that is tearing creation apart. The gentle butterfly reminds me of my journey through love and joy and peace. Butterflies flit from flower to flower giving gentle kisses. Active during daytime, they bring joy to our transforming souls with each flutter of their wings.

Butterflies have four wings that move up and down in a figure-eight pattern. Their pattern is associated with continuity of infinity of life. Christians use the butterfly as a symbol of spiritual transformation. Native Americans do a butterfly dance as their expression of thanksgiving for the ongoing cycle of new seasons and new life. They dance with a bright colored shawl which represents butterfly wings.

As the butterfly flies along with no thought of its old life, we trust the strength of our new spiritual wings to carry us into eternal life. Butterflies have compound eyes with thousands of lenses. They can even see ultraviolent light. Butterflies calls us to balance, personal growth, clear and complete vision of our inner souls, so that we stay connected to the spirit as we walk through the changes in our own life journeys.

My own visit with a butterfly that landed on my shoe reminded me of my gentle brother offering assurance that all was well with him.

Native American tribes view the butterfly as a messenger to the Great Spirit. They believe that if a butterfly lands on a person, that person can whisper a prayer. They prayer will fly to heaven in the butterfly wings, carrying them to the Great Spirit.

A group of butterflies are called a flutter. The group reminds us that life holds playful joy. The flutter calls us to open our eyes to the beauty discovered every day. This ephemeral being connects our souls to love.

Germans have told me that children would draw butterflies on their prison walls in the Nazi death camps.

The butterfly is my perfect symbol of gentleness. Colossians 3:9-10. God places butterflies in many places throughout creation. Reflecting on their gentle ways gives me spiritual wisdom. Despite the sacrifices a caterpillar makes, retreating for a season and then stepping out into the unknown. Imagine what it gains. Beautiful wings that enable it to fly and to reach places and go distances it never could before its transformation.

Torpy Skinner, a woman from Tennessee, wrote about a time when received a chrysalis inside a clear jar. She and her daughter watched and saw wings inside. They took the jar outside when the butterfly was halfway out. It stood on the rim of the jar. It wobbled as it hesitated before attempting to fly.

The gentle creature flew up and down almost hitting the ground. Suddenly, the butterfly soared away.

Skinner noted that humans are like that when we live through major changes such as moving into a new job, home, church, or school. We wobble with uncertainty in our efforts to adjust. As we keep working at it, we eventually settle into our new way of life. We look back at our own lives and recognize the times when we were like a butterfly. With our new wings, we shall soar into gentle, joyful, and loving creatures of God.

Changes are difficult, but God us strength as we encounter ups and downs. (Torpy Skinner, "Navigating Changes," *The Upper Room*, September-October 2022, p. 31)

There are places God wants us to take us. Do you hear God's gentle voice? We must be transformed by the renewing of our minds. Romans 12:1-2. Allow God to transform us, so we can reach higher levels of faith and gentleness.

.

A Gentle Conversation with God

James, it was me that caused the butterfly to rest gently on your shoe after you brother David joined Me in heaven. I am filled with joy because My butterfly spoke to you.

It is part of the mystery of how our expectations are supposed to be altered. I can use any situation such as the mystery of the caterpillar becoming a butterfly. I know you got it.

My children do change often. Butterflies remind you of how something so magnificent comes from My ordinary caterpillars and my ordinary adopted sons and daughters.

Now you know that I can work miracles in any life situation. I was the one who inspired Dolly Parton to write and sing "Love is like a butterfly."

It is I who gives the gift of gentleness. I am with you as you live through the ups and downs of life.

Gentleness in the Compassion

"Mr. Rogers" demonstrated gentleness as compassion from his television pulpit. He was an ordained Presbyterian minister, who impacted millions of people around the world. Mr. Rogers summed up his message. "Most of us, I believe, admire strength. It's something we tend to respect in others, desire for ourselves, and wish for our children.

"Sometimes I wonder if we confuse strength and other words like aggression and violence. Real strength is neither male nor female; but is, quite simply, one of the finest characteristics that any human being can possess." (Maxwell King, *Good Neighbor: The Life and Work of Fred Rogers*, pp. 16-17)

Mr. Rogers was introverted and sensitive who ministered against the grain of the noise of the world. "Mister Rogers' Neighborhood" glued millions to sit still as they watched.

Mr. Rogers was discovered by a new generation when Tom Hanks played Mr. Rogers in a movie about his life. He wore a tie and a cardigan. He parted his hair on the left like an office clerk. He had a rare genius for communicating with children. He listened to kids. He conveyed to them a powerful respect.

On one of his shows, he invited a boy with cerebral palsy This gentle host ask for the boy's help by praying. Mr. Rogers asked because he had gone through many challenges must be close to God. (Ibid., pp. 96-119)

Gentleness absorbs the shocks from unavoidable collisions. With compassion, it observes, slows down, and plugs in. Gentleness is alive to the need of the moment. Gentleness never rests on its laurels. It never assumes that the compassionate response today is the one needed for tomorrow.

It is a soft supportive pillow. We recognize it when we see it in action. Compassion means "to suffer together." We are seen, heard, and never alone. Rarely being able to see people as people, we have a chronic lack of gentleness. So, we never look in compassion with any depth.

Compassion is gentle because it digs deeper than our conditioned exteriors. Gentleness is like the power of water. The persistent flow over time gives us life. Water carves through mountains as it defines who we are as humans.

Nothing is as gentle as ocean waves lapping at the shore. Billions of years went into setting the scenes for the moments of today. Water's rhythmic repetition carves the miracles in the world. Gentleness is like that.

Gentleness is compassionately holding each other. Joy is the spark of connection within ourselves and between us. The operational definition of gentleness is showing personal compassion in meeting needs of others." Compassionate people have experienced God's love. Compassion requires wisdom to discern what level of involvement is appropriate. Wisdom steps in to empathize with a person's need and to take suitable action. Gentleness is the final touch, carrying out the act of compassion in a thoughtful and tender manner.

Lacking gentleness, intentions cause more harm than good. God's loving tenderness helps us minister to others. II Corinthians 1:4. Jesus is the example. Like a shepherd who cares for the sheep, God cares for us in times of distress. Psalm 23:1-4. Jesus was known for the gentleness of his words, even with those who rejected him. Jesus valued little children and blessed those who were brought to him. Mark 10: 14-16. Jesus demonstrated gentleness when he raised a young girl to life. He aided the grieving parents by keeping the crowd outside. Luke 8:49-55.

Compassion is not what society gives to those caught up in an indiscretion. We remember Marilyn, Monica, and so many powerful people lure each other into inappropriate relationships.

Donna Rice was enchanted with Gary Hart, a presidential hopeful in 1987. Their romantic overtures led to public scandal. Donna accompanied Hart, a married man, on a pleasure cruise to the Bahamas. She was a wholesome and attractive woman.

When the news media got hold of the story, both lovers were devastated. The slowly developing but passionate affair, left both twisted by their compromises. Rice and the nation saw her picture on the front pages of newspapers and magazines all over the world.

For a while, her life fell apart. Her family and friends were shocked, and they had no compassion. She resigned her job. She kept being hounded by the press. She was offered millions to tell her story. Enemies of Gary Hart were eager to further hurt him. She wrestled with what to do. Her parents and her grandmother told Rice: "Before you make any decisions, get your life straight with God."

Rice was confused and stunned. Both tried to patch together their marriages. Both continued to be unhappy. Compassion and gentleness were not to be found. After several years, she received a message from a friend. She told Rice, "Donna, I can imagine you are in a lot of pain. I want you know that God loves you and your true friends love you."

Rice recalls, "My friend shared some songs we used to sing together. I had sobbed many times over my life plight. Nobody else including Gary Hart, were responsible for my decisions." (Craig Brian Larson and Brian Lowery, *Engaging Illustrations for Preachers,* pp. 29-34)

Gentleness in the compassion for others works miracles. Who are we to judge? We might to do anything the same way if we thought we could.

Love is the mechanism of gentleness. Words and actions are powerful. They can both hurt and heal. The way we speak encourages others. Gentleness is for earthen vessels who shuffle along with feet of clay.

Jesus came for the sake of those who fail. He came as a friend to the friendless. His message mended broken hearts. He comforts those who mourn. He is the hero for the helpless.

Gentle joy causes one to be teachable. Teachableness means willingness to learn. Compassion is being considerate. Showing consideration, calmness, caring, and bearing with others out of our love. Ruth Gendler, who says of herself that the hermit attempts to overshadow her aspects of solitude. Her writing is creative. She writes of compassion: "Compassion speaks with a slight accent. She was a vulnerable child, miserable in school, cold, sly, alert to the pain in the eyes of her sturdier classmates. The other kids teased her about being too sentimental and gentle, and for a long time she believed them. In ninth grade she was befriended by Courage.

"Courage lent Compassion bright sweaters, explained the slang, showed her how to play volleyball, taught her you can love people and not care what they think about you.

"In many ways Compassion is still the stranger, neither wonderful, nor terrible, herself, utterly, always." (J. Ruth Gendler, *The Book of Qualities*, p. 23).

Compassion is the opposite of harshness Weakness or inferiority have no place. Being compassionate is spiritual and is the foundation for power. I Timothy 6:11. Tenderness is not being weak. Compassion is fortitude. Solidarity and humility are basic for dealing with others' failing and faults. Gentle compassion is the true sign of divine power. A shepherd has a crook, a staff where she can pull back one of the sheep who has strayed. He never beats the sheep. The staff is not used to hurt the sheep. The sheep follow freely.

A person who was not familiar with farming sheep once related that he had made a trip to Europe He talked about a man forcing and compelling sheep, the flock, into a pen. He was pushing them, beating them, whacking them across their rear ends. He was aggressively forcing them into the pen.

The farmer said, "Now, wait a minute. What you saw was not a shepherd. He was the butcher. The butcher beats the sheep into the pen, and then butchers them. A shepherd does not butcher sheep. He never beats them. He never sticks the end of his staff into their bodies.

He calls each sheep by name. They follow freely. They follow voluntarily. They are proud to be members of his flock. Once we embrace God's unlimited love and strength, we live in trust not fear. God is the good shepherd whose response to our butchering is tender mercy. Jesus is the human face of God. Some people live in utter fear. The result is transference of fear onto God.

We are not better than anybody. We are always to be gentle even when we have been wronged. Gentleness is loving God and others. We must continue to work on ourselves for this gentle joy to be a possibility. Repeat again and again how God is gentle with us. Incorporate gentleness into life.

Through the privilege of prayer, we are given a spirit of gentleness. Ask God to take away our self-righteousness. Be willing to be loving. We can ask God to reveal the ways we can demonstrate gentleness to other so we might become reflectors of the character of God.

Before the fullness of joy comes, we recognize where we have fallen short. In that place where we were wounded, God touches us to be compassionately joy gentle. God touches us and causes us to walk humbly. We are grateful and we express our thanks.

Without sincere repentance, joy is a hollow and fragile shell. In spite of the weaknesses, we know are within us, we must keep seeking examples of God's compassion with love. Stretch your new experience that show how to express it.

Feel divine Spirit within you. The Holy Spirit is love. With the Spirit's guidance and direction, love and compassion will ooze out from us overflowing. Compassion is possible.

God's compassionate, self-giving love treats every human being as special. No ideology that would tempt you to trespass the character of God. Just love God as we love ourselves.

Soak in that love and compassion. Living water will reach to the roots of our being. The water from God will refresh, touch, heal, and cleanse. Love yourself enough to let the love fill you and me. Love will unlock doors guarded by our guilt. Forgiveness opens the doors sin has closed.

A Gentle Conversation with God

Jim, I have compassion for you. The fact that I have always covered you in gentleness while you were actively wrong, should tell you just Who I am.

If you will choose to take on My ways, gentleness toward others who are sinners may offer a door to them that being sternness never could.

Often My disciples make loud noises of praise without recognizing the nature of Who I am. They honor Jesus with their lips, but they have no compassion. I offer you peace and rest with deep compassion. Be an ever-renewed source of My peace.

Go to a quiet place where you can hear My voice.

Look, there are evil forces in this world. They are destructive and unkind. As you show compassion to people, even within the church, these spirits must be confronted, silenced, and commanded to leave. Jesus will be with you there as you attempt to silence them.

Gentleness in the Bible

Gentleness is the most overlooked fruit of the Spirit. The Bible has much to say about gentleness. There are many examples. Jesus is the best model. Before we begin to unpack what having gentleness means, we look at its meaning. Gentleness is defined as the quality of being tender, kind, compassionate, and considerate. To have gentleness is to have a gentle nature. Gentleness means to show love and care for others by the way we act and speak. Proverbs 2:1-6.

Gentleness is shown in the Old Testament as a stream or river. Isaiah 8:6. It is illustrated by a shepherd caring for his flock of lambs. It is a soft touch, a loving hand, and calm reassurance.

In the New Testament Jesus is the perfect example of "being gentle and humble of heart." Matthew 11:29. Paul continues to model gentleness as he proclaims and writes about the good news. I Thessalonians 2:7, I Corinthians 4:21.

Scripture shows a strong connection between gentleness and the power of words. Proverbs indicates that gentle words turn away wrath. Proverbs 15:1. The power of our words is life-giving. They diffuse a tense situation.

In sharing the gospel, we are to be gentle and respectful. I Peter 3:15-16. We are to speak the truth but to watch our tone so the truth will be well received. Gentleness is important. We will be blessed and rewarded by God by receiving peace now and with God in heaven. Truth, beauty, and goodness are precious Bible treasures. Digging deeper into the word of God, we realize who God is. We allow God to work in us as a radiant expression of love.

The Bible shows the ways to show gentleness. We are asked to be considerate of others' needs and feelings. We are to demonstrate empathy. Empathy is to acknowledge another's point of view. Seek peace. Search for common ground for solutions. Remember the Golden Rule. Treat others as you wish to be treated. Be a calm presence. Listen more than we speak. James 1:19. Act with tenderness and love. Be humble as we serve. Be patient. Ephesians 4:2. Read these scriptures and Colossians 3:12, I Timothy 6:11, Proverbs 15:1, 4, Ephesians 4:2, Titus 3:1-2 in your favorite or accurate translation. (Dallas Willard, *The Allure of Gentleness: Defending the Faith in the Manner of Jesus*, pp. 203-209)

God is glorified as we take on divine character. The Holy Spirit tenderly guides our prayer when we don't know our need or how to ask. Romans 8:26.

The Bible reveals how we can be gentle. We must follow Christ's example of leading gently. Isaiah 40:11. Our though life yields pleasant words. Proverbs 15:26. We don't jump to conclusions. We listen patiently before we speak. James 1:19-20. We are tenderhearted and forgiving of offenders. Ephesians 4:31-32.

Jesus describes himself as "gentle and humble." We struggle to draw close to God because we do not understand his gentleness. The Bible gives us insight into what gentleness is and what it is not. We can explore internal and external hindrances to embracing the gentleness of God. Scripture teaches that being gentle recognizes that God's thoughts and ways are high above our own. Isaiah 55:9.

God is omniscient. We are not. Gentleness means giving up the right to judge what is best for others and for us. We accept that the rain falls on the evil and the just. Let God be in control. This invitation is broad. Matthew 11:28. Jesus is gentle with the weary and those who carry heavy burdens.

Before the arrival of Jesus, the children of God lived a hopeless time. Matthew 11:29. Gentleness is a strong hand with a soft touch. God cares for the defenseless. Isaiah 40:11. The tender nature of God causes the most critical ones to soften. Gentleness goes a long way in reaching critics. II Corinthians 10:1.

Studying the Bible assures us that God does not change. Even under intense suffering or joyous delight, God is God.

We all far short of the biblical ideal for gentleness. I certainly know that I do. Romans 7:15. We hold onto our boastful souls, prideful attitudes, and harsh words. The Church tips its hat to gentleness, but in our practice, pride wins out.

As an author and seeker, I pray these words in this

book will settle in the deepest parts of our souls and that gentle joy takes root for the sake of Jesus. I continue to believe that the Bible can help us, as we journey in God's love.

Psalm 18:35. "Your gentleness makes me great." Is David the psalmist being arrogant? As I studied this word more, I found "gentleness" can mean condescension. Our souls magnify God when they acknowledge their lowly position. Understanding gentleness begins in the gospels. Matthew 11:29, 21:5.

Nobody becomes gentle on their own. Gentleness requires death to us in our living. It is powerful strength under control. We need not dispute with God or resist love. Christ has already done the hardest part. With love, grace, and gentleness, God allows people like us to participate in the beautiful fruit to be gentle.

Prayer is the oil. Rejoicing is the natural result. Gentleness is wrapped in joy and prayer. We must be teachable. James 3:13. Jesus voluntarily condescended from the eternal throne to rescue us from certain infinite death.

Our lives lived in front of a watching world reveals our integrity. We focus on the eternal, not the perishable. Christ makes us beautiful. I Peter 3:3-4. We get caught up in the outward, the external. The world encourages this. The outer human is decaying. Consideration can be translated gentleness in Titus 3:2. We are to demonstrate, show, and prove our gentleness.

Jesus assures us that the gentle will inherit the earth. The actions of God as recorded in the Holy Scriptures assures us of divine reality in our own life journeys. In teaching Luke-Acts for my church groups, I noted that everything that has been written as occurring in the early church is a small part of what the Spirit of God was giving throughout the entire world.

Christian scribes gave us no insight of the missions in North Africa. No mention of the evangelion in India where Thomas established congregations that have continued in the thousands of Thomism churches that share the gospel today. There are no canonical scriptures about the ministries in Gaul, modern day France, or Spain. Antioch, the third largest city in the Roman Empire, received a bare mention. Antioch was where followers of Christ were first called Christians out of derision.

A Gentle Conversation with God

Hey Jim, My beloved. I have plucked the fruit of gentleness from the tree of life, and now I hand it to you as My gift. It's gentleness that includes the way for moral excellence, goodness, kindness, and usefulness.

Today is a new opportunity to practice growing in gentleness. Learn about Me in the scriptures. When you approach your sisters and brothers in Christ who may be different from you, it appears impossible to bridge the gap. Each person has an opinion striving for victory over the others.

My gentleness is available to you to persist in seeking My Spirit to heal the differences. In the hurting places, I am with you. I am with you to give you courage and to enable you to come through the duress and confusion. I know you sense your own weakness as you read My Word.

I am with you always.

Gentleness in the World

Gentleness is not found in our societal imagination. We cultivate virtues in our own image. My research for scholarly works on gentleness yielded very little. We need to resurrect gentleness more than ever. Yet, there is no room for it in our imagined would-be kingdoms.

Gentleness and firmness have gone together. The French say, "One must have hands of steel in gloves of velvet." The world has defined gentleness. Xenophon (434-355 B.C.) was a historian and a soldier. He defined gentleness as the brotherly understanding which develops between soldiers who have been fighting together for a long time.

Plato (427-347 B.C.) was a Greek philosopher. His use of gentleness was a sense of politeness and courtesy. It holds human society together. He used the term to describe a tamed thoroughbred who uses its strength for a master's desires.

Socrates (470-399 B.C.) used the term to mean the comparison of gentleness and scolding.

Aristotle (384-322 B.C.) was another Greek philosopher whose thoughts are shared in a basic philosophy class. To him, gentleness is a balance between too much anger and not enough anger, or an incapacity to feel anger. It was the proper self-control of anger. He noted that anger should be expressed against evil. (Christopher Peterson and Martin

Seligman, *Character Strengths and Virtues: A Handbook and Classification,* pp. 32-45)

In the world, people are not sensitive to gentleness. Comedian Pete Davidson mocked congressman-elect Dan Crenshaw because of his eye patch. Crenshaw lost his eye as a Navy Seal in Iraq. There was a stinging public backlash against Davidson. Davidson was so devastated he became deeply depressed. He no longer wished to live. Crenshaw reached out to comedian Pete. He said that everyone has a purpose in this world. Live that purposeful way.

Instead of condemning, Dan built a bridge. Instead of shaming, Crenshaw responded with tenderness. Instead of seeking vindication, he sought friendship. Instead of adding to the outrage, he gave unconditional love. This gentle spirit requires the most heroic faith. Faithfulness such as this is possible only through the gentle power of Christ.

The world rewards the powerful. They rely on their own power to grab what they want in life. And it works. Those who chase power never take time to look in the rearview mirror. They fail to recognize the mass of hurting people that have been consumed along the pathway to the top.

Instead of being kind and tender, the world hurdles over others to get to the front of the line. God calls us to submit our hearts and our intentions that gentleness is the way to real success.

If we are authentically gentle, we are not attempting to gain control over someone or something. Gentlemen and gentlewomen are free to be more compassionate, helpful, loving and supportive.

If our world would follow Jesus, then the world recognizes and uses his teachings in all gentleness is not an option. The gentle ones do not find strength in ways culture has privileged them in most fields including church positions. The exhortation to be gentle is modeled by Jesus. It has been implored in faith since the time of Christ.

To seek out gentleness is counter-cultural to the ins and outs of daily existence. The world does not cherish humility. Gentleness can only grow in the soil of humility. And it starts with me and you. II Timothy 2:24-26.

We crave the salve of more softness, generosity of spirit, gentleness. Becoming intentionally gentler is a rebellion in our world that is increasingly too mean. Too polarized. Too rude. Too full of agonism. Too much overstimulation. Too full. Too unhealthy. The new normal in the world is anything but gentle. Hatefulness. Roughness. Harshness. Agitation. Soften self-talk. Repeat, "Gentle is my superpower. Gentle is strength." (Robert J. Weeks, *Living a Gentle and Passionate Life*, p. 139-154)

Imagine the family, the workplace, the friends, and communities if we gave others gentleness. Imagine being open to a gentler relationship with ourselves, each other, and with our world. We would be less defensive, more accepting, and less leaning on the old narratives. We would face our challenges, injustices, fears, inner battles. Overlearning gentleness to the uttermost becomes by default quite liberating. Energy is contagious. Without gentleness, we close ourselves off to optimal learning, to each other, to healthy vulnerability.

We relax our boundaries. We are joyously surprised at what begins to flow in our lives. Gentleness is big enough to hold all of us. The world is afraid of the dark. Conditional belonging threatens us. The sad result is violence. Gentleness weeps at that dilemma which keeps us isolated and not part of the beautiful whole. The whole world benefits from us being filled with alertness.

Compassion includes play. Play uses curiosity and wonder. Playful people push away their pride. They counter the heart of cynicism. Gentleness holds space for every one of us. It is reassuring. Compassionate gentleness keeps us trying, growing, and experiencing encouragement. The world can then emerge and unite sowing seeds for our future together.

When we are held gently, we feel safe. We relax. We are not tense and anxious. Compassionate and gentle people work in partnership, not in opposition.

Anne Dufourmantelle was a French philosopher who wrote about her version of the power of gentleness. She wrote that gentleness is a difficult term to define. How can we conceptualize gentleness? What philosophical import, what potential for human action and thought does gentleness contain?" (Anne Dufourmantelle, *Power of Gentleness: Meditations on the Risk of Living*, pp. 54-56)

The answer for the first question is that gentleness cannot be defined. It eludes capture with thoughts and words. She has the concept that "gentleness" comes first as a failure. (Ibid., p. 54) To her, failure is the starting point for beginning to answer what power resides in gentleness, where sweetness turns to resistance.

Her text pulls together scholarly thoughts from Tolstoy, Gandhi, Melville, Nietzsche, Hildegard of Bingen. In the well-written foreword by Catherine Malabou wrote: "This book is not only written about gentleness, and in some sense written by gentleness, a gentleness revealing itself, but is itself gentle." (Anne Dufourmantelle, *Power of Gentleness: Meditations on Risk Living*, foreword, pp. ii-v)

Her work is worth reading. Her book is in French, but also a language of the wind, a breeze, a warm current that carries the whisper of another way of existing She teaches with risk. Her thoughts are quite difficult to understand or write about, both elusive and allusive. (Ibid., pp. 70-85)

We know little about gentleness from science. There are few research projects in the past on this subject. It has been popular with ministers and with people in church circles. The world needs a strong definition of what gentleness is. That would require a validated measurement as a tool to access it.

Gentleness is a compound character trait. It cannot be boiled down to a single strength. There are multiple strengths. No combination captures the nuances of that. Science has tried to find combination strengths in studying respect, patience, responsibility, mindfulness, tolerance, and encouragement.

In the world unspeakably darkened by crisis, it appears trifling to devote our attention to beauty in this world. Beauty is a redemptive process. It is like putting a broken vase back together. (Ella Francis Sanders, *Everything Beautiful: A Guide to Finding Hidden Beauty in the World,* pp. 6-44)

Ella Sanders expands and upends our notions of beauty and urges us to notice the ingredients for beauty all around us. Sanders writes about the way to spread gentleness.

My dad and mother told me and my brothers, "Always, boys, be gentle to yourselves and others. Gentleness has a great impact on the world." My parents were poor, but gentleness made them rich.

As we consider the mentality in the world, we notice that gentleness is not a common term. Most live by missing the mark through irresponsibility, fornication, idolatry, feuds, jealousy, bad tempers, disagreements, envy, and similar actions. Gentleness is ignored and despised. According to the apostle Paul, gentleness is a prime characteristic of the world of the Spirit. The touch of gentleness is present in every one of the fruits of the spirit.

Jesus taught us to be gentler. We are called to be gentle with all the people who live with us in the world. God is always gentle to everyone on the earth. In one of my conversations with our gentle Lord, I tried to process my disturbances at the reality of the world. As I was doing that, stopped to listen in silence.

God asked me, "How do I treat you?" My humble answer was, "Always with gentleness and love." I always enjoy my quiet times with God. That particular day, I heard God communicating to me, "Act the same with all people."

A Gentle Conversation with God

Jim, I notice you are writing another book. It pleases me that you have used your gifts from me to glorify and honor me. You have been a gentle child of mine. You remind me somewhat of Paul. Read his thoughts in I Thessalonians 2:7-8.

Those who came to know Me through you will be responsive to your tender concerns. I look out for your daughter and grandson for whom you have shared yourself. I am pleased to be your Father.

You have been open, honest, vulnerable, and loving toward others. By now, everyone whom I sent into your path knows that as minister of joy to My world you are frail, sinful, passionate, and naïve. You have persistently held onto Me. I sent personal angels to protect you.

By now you must realize that I sent My angels to save you from certain death. Sometimes it takes a long time for truth, beauty, and goodness to prevail. Time is needed for some changes. My unconditional love for you does not involve "twiddling My thumbs" or stamping about with worried impatience. Mine is the way of loving the whole world that as you believe in Me, you will enjoy eternal life.

Gentleness in the Workplace

Gentleness is an underestimated power in the workplace. While I was serving Saint Luke United Methodist Church in Bristol, Virginia, I visited an extraordinary couple. They opened up their home to take in young people who lacked one. These youth were too old to be placed in a foster home. They have provided single moms with their newborns. The couple pictures gestures of gentleness. They always gave a gentle answer to each question.

Workplaces must understand the nature of workplace conflict. Consequences of conflict, side from personal insults, attacks, and bullying, included organizational level impact such as absence from work, employee turnover, and project failures.

Most of us who have served in manipulating, mean-spirited companies identify. This inability to resolve conflicts at work is keeping multitudes awake at night. Gentleness is a conscious choice. We can act harsh and uppity. Or we can be gentle with our smiles, welcoming arms, soft voice tones, and inviting words.

Gentleness requires a shift away from ego and selfish interests. We must focus less on self and more on others. Hire people who care for others and enjoy helping others succeed. The workplace must be a safe and nurturing environment. Workplace supervisors restore dignity and confidence in their workers.

Spirit of Joy churches, schools, and healthy workplaces are linked to our collective relationship with gentleness. Businesses are quick to reject gentleness because gentleness is a threat to the world, we say we do not want but we are afraid of changing in any meaningful way.

Gentleness is a firm back with a soft front. The world would become a paradise for all people if we could conceive of gentleness as compassion, as joy, as big enough to hold all of us, as a place of safety and creativity, as the universalizing connection.

Gentleness makes a huge difference in our work lives. We might be surprised how ungentle we are. Without realizing it, as we hurry to do things quickly. We tend to drop things. We must start again. We always must do things more than once. This hurried approach causes us to be less considerate of our fellow workers.

Practicing gentleness in the workplace creates an atmosphere where work is done better and quicker. The richest rewards were far beyond earning a paycheck. Gentleness is the key to freedom from anger, apathy, and aggression.

The power behind gentleness is God. Divine power. Personality clashes and warring egos are the primary cause of workplace conflict. We must discover the power in gentleness. It touches hearts. It changes people from within the deep places. It is better to influence others through gentleness rather than force. When bosses use forceful tactics, work is done with resistance. Fear and punishment inhibit work.

Somebody said, "Gentleness doesn't get work done unless you are a chicken laying eggs." Workers might act nice, but the niceness might be to cover the fear.

Gentleness is not the opposite of strength or passion. Gentle people do not break fragile people. Gentleness is when the stronger ones restrain their strength for the sake of the weaker. Difficult workplaces, unreasonable bosses, and disappointments stir in the videos in my mind. Those memories are still fresh in my soul as I wrestle with how to write about gentleness. Writing about gentleness is difficult because being gentle is not complicated. There is nothing to explain. Writers do not need to scold or berate the readers with examples of the lack of gentleness. Any writer who complicates is really trying to create excuses for their lack of gentleness.

Hurricanes help us understand power without control. Entire nations demonstrate uncontrolled power. Gentleness is the most overlooked fruit in the workplace. Church has been my place of work. I found that the highly organized church does not honor gentleness. Boasting is practically an art form. Culture glorifies the powerful. The Church tends to gravitate towards leaders who are self-confident and prideful. Jesus said that he is "gentle and lowly in heart." Matthew 11:29. Jesus is not harsh. He was not reactionary. He was not easily exasperated.

The love of God leads us to gentleness. It was listed by Paul near the end because it is most challenging to be developed in our workplaces. The workplace is not to tear down others. Gentleness generates from a relationship with God. Gentleness is a form of grace. Galatians 6:1-2.

Being spiritual means being gentle with others. Secular companies hire people of many religious faiths and those with no faith. They must respect the holy days of all faiths. "Right to work" in most places means the company has the right to fire or to destroy the economic or personal life of workers.

Each time we enter a new workplace, we realize that God needed us to representatives of the kingdom of God in just the right places at just the right time. Some quit their jobs and relocate from a theological and biblical perspective.

The initial anxiety-producing situation is meeting the boss. Like a box of chocolates, you never know what you get. When we apply for jobs, nothing is as it seems. This is a challenge for all workers as we have heard of, seen, or have had terrible bosses. Negativity has been in every workplace since Adam and Eve. Work becomes painful.

Starting a new job requires us to see the boss as someone whom God has put in your journey for a variety of reasons. Their sinful attitudes and actions are part of the "thorns and thistles" that we experience.

Figuring out new job responsibilities is the next challenge to be faced. This one is just a little less scary than the new boss. We have some insight into what we are getting into than we would be if we had not worked before. Your employer hands you more projects than we can handle. Some accept jobs of which they are overqualified. There is no challenge. With all our education and preparation, we just do not fit.

In addition to our own struggles with a new boss and a new job, our family does not understand as we are required to focus our time and energy on our work. God provides some of our employment in which we fail.

God put us where we are for more than a paycheck. Perhaps we learn something that is critical for our future.

Whatever the reason that we work in new assignments we know God will use us. God will be present with you as you use the talents and gifts we possess. We will always discover joy as we remember the past work when we leave. We know that every job was a significant part of abundant eternal life.

A Gentle Conversation with God

The discipline for My followers requires a willingness to go through hardship in order to obey My guidance. My Spirit may lead to many jobs and workplaces so you can grow and develop and lay down your own agenda.

One day every worker's eye will be opened, and they will see Me as I am. The world's workers will look Me into My eyes.

Keep looking for miracles that nudge you in the direction of My flowing current. In this world of gray, My standard for the workplace is clear when you search Me and My Word. Read III John 11.

All the bosses and the workers must continue measuring themselves according to My standards and policies.

The responsibility I place on your shoulders and the workers who know the truth. You are responsible simply because you know what the right thing is to do. Keep on asking for my love. I promise to be with you every day of your life.

Gentleness in the Ministry

After my platinum jubilee of 70 years in ministry, I wonder if I accomplished anything by devoting myself to preaching, teaching, writing, and counseling. When I talk or write about something such as gentleness. Immediately afterward somebody within my audience acts or speaks in a way that's condemning and harsh. My words fall to the church floor as people leave.

Ministers, ordained or not, are called to imitate the gentleness of Jesus. Gentleness is the quality of being mild, tender, and kind. We hear people speak of a gentle reminder, a gentle breeze, or a gentle stream of water.

Even as serving as a minister, we find that gentleness is not a quality to be desired. Being gentle in the current climate of the church is impossible. James 3:13. It is sad that many pastors and prominent leaders are so obviously lacking in gentleness.

Paul told us to let our gentleness be known to everyone. People are always looking at us. We learn by what we experience and see. When a minister sins, there is no mercy. Galatians 6:1-2. The church is the only army that shoots its wounded. The pastor does not trust telling his supervisor or bishop about her mistakes. The church is the last place many people will turn when they have seriously messed by their lives. They feel badly enough.

The apostle Paul says that a Holy Spirit led minister has the ability to minister to the fallen. Ministers restore someone in a spirit of gentleness. Every action of a called and ordained servant must be gentle. The signs of quality of our spiritual lives include gentleness, tranquility, and strength with which we deal with the circumstances that inevitably show up.

The stronger one becomes, the gentler she will be. Belittling. Name calling. Harshness. Bullying. These things must be controlled. Gentleness is strengths harnessed and channeled to produce God's desire for each human being. Gentleness flows from the recognition that we too are tempted to leave the path Jesus walks.

The motto for Carson-Newman University is "truth, beauty, goodness." The school now has a reputation for rigorous scholarship with a commitment to truth. They care about the beauty of each student's soul. Some of the brightest and creative ministers prepared for ministry at this Southern Baptist institution. Everyone is required to take Bible and religion classes. Even the science, language, and all who teach there follow Jesus with gentleness, goodness, kindness, tenderness, and humility.

Gentleness matters. It is rare and precious. It is in short supply. Ministers are called to share the good news to people who are aggressive, harsh, combative, judgmental, and mean. This comes without surprise. Gentleness is not a trait that this world values. My book is a rare one if you look in bookstores.

If we hear that a church congregation has selected a new senior minister who was gentle, not many will flock to hear her or him. Gentleness should be a major qualification for doing ministry. Paul said an elder must be "not violent, but gentle." Titus 1:7. We "speak the truth in love." Ephesians 4:15.

God has been gentle with us. That is what makes Christian ministry so amazing. Those who sacrifice time, money, pleasure, other opportunities are unique, different, and special.

There is a tight bond between Christ and the church. When a shepherd does not display the gentle nature of Jesus, this shatters the sheep's perception of this identification of Christ with the Church. A minister is a servant of the head of the church. Matthew 23:8-12. In this scripture, Jesus pronounced eight woes on spiritual leaders because they were not right with God.

Ministers exhibit gentleness in caring for sinners. Immeasurable comfort is found in Christ. Lacking Christlike gentleness, ministers often do a poor job of ministering to the deepest hurts. When displaying love and care, we are the hands and feet of Christ. As Martin Luther put it, "The higher people are in the favor of God, the more tender they are." A person with a short temper who resorts to aggression and anger is not strong in any sense.

Gentleness and strength coexist. Saint Francis de Sales said to priests, "Nothing is so strong as gentleness. Nothing is so gentle as real strength."

Gentleness is the act of being kind and tender. Ministers (and all Christians are ministers) create calm, peace, and contentment. Gentleness is sensitive by nature. Strength cultivates resilience, confidence, and assertiveness.

Ministers need to be strong enough to not internalize criticism from a superior or congregational leader. Leaders need to be strong. They will have to withstand hardships. Seminary professors need to warn students about the fact of what a minister will face as a leader, and not create the impression that ministry is a romantic venture filled with laurels. Every leader has a breaking point. Strength understands emotions. When we allow ourselves to feel, emotions will not overcome you. The mental state affects what we achieve in life.

How ministers treat themselves affects how they do their best. We push ourselves beyond any human limits. Ministry is not an easy calling. At times it is extremely uncomfortable. During our journey, we will make mistakes, get unjustly critiqued, and accept failure. Self-compassion keeps us from beating ourselves inside.

Being polite and mindful of your manners to avoid being ignorant or rude. My English professor at Carson-Newman, Agnes Hull, taught a special class on proper manners and how to come off as one who can go anywhere in the world and be comfortable. She drove me to church with her to the First Baptist Church in Knoxville and introduced me to Charles Trentham, a gentle and encouraging pastor.

There are so many simple but essential things to know and do if one would serve in church leadership. Avoid being impatient. Help or assist whenever it's possible. Cheerfully serve. Choose your words carefully. Give and accept constructive criticisms. Notice inner reactions. Gather information with curiosity.

Imagine a loving color of light moving between people through words and expressions. Let the color come when speaking or encountering another. That is loving in between. The toughest relationship is within us. The most overlooked and underrated trait of people who serve in healthy, growing churches is gentleness.

Go to any church doing great things for the kingdom of God year after year. Smell the joy and excitement in the air. Show me a church served by control freaks, the easily offended, the seldom laughing, and I will show you a church in decline. The best articulated vision will be eaten for breakfast. No pastor can execute a vision without a supportive church culture.

If we sincerely want to know what gentleness is, then we best study the one who declared, "I am gentle." Matthew 11:29. Gentleness is a matter of conduct. Jesus did not say to act gentle. Jesus acts gentle because he is gentle.

The connection between gentleness and humility is the frequent refrain of the New Testament. Jesus knew that to be effective in his ministry, he had to bring himself low, to temper his might with gentleness. His gentle ways are strength sacrificially tempered by love. Ministry is eagerly directed towards bearing the burdens of others.

We get insight in Matthew 21:1-11 when Jesus sends his disciples to fetch a donkey that he might ride into Jerusalem. Scripture tells us that this odd request took place to fulfill the prophecy of Zechariah 9:9. There is no clearer demonstration of gentleness.

"Thank God for your work, which is one of the blessings of your life. Then wait patiently in the silence and listen. Let the Spirit speak to your heart about new ways of approaching what you do." (John Killinger, *Prayer: The Act of Being with God*, pp. 64-65.)

A Gentle Conversation with God

Jim, I remember many wonderful things as we have known and loved each other. I have come to you for bring salvation. You know, my called minister of joy, that it is not enough to simply rest in our relationship.

I your God knows about your healthy discontent until I can find a way and a place to share this gentleness with others. They are floundering, unable to discern the Rescuer because of the troubled waters. Part of my gentleness is enabling ministers such as you to be part of my rescue team.

Gentleness in the Family

In the videos of my family memories, I remember the gentle touches of my mother and my dad. Watching television or reading, I would lay my head in their laps, and I felt my parents' gently stroking my arms or back. When I got sick, I felt their cool, soft hands on my forehead or on my chest to put on a concoction that was a family tradition. They prayed for me and assured me that I would become well.

I want my friends and family to remember my touch as gentle. I cherish the sight of people whose embrace and hug are so tender that they inspire me to cultivate my own gentle touch. Holding our children and grandchildren is soft, real, intentional, and careful tenderness. When my daughter was about four years old, her mother called me in my office to say that my daughter was upset because I had forgotten to give her a bye-bye kiss. There was a winter storm and I had walked to work. The little kiss was so important that I walked back home.

Gentleness connects us on a deeper level of intimacy. Our loved ones know that we cherish their feelings. It brings healing to tension or misunderstandings. We express our love and caring in ways that are appreciated, understood, and received. There have been times when a gentle glance and a smile says everything. Gratefulness for something someone has done makes a special connection. There is an overflow of dignity in gentle people.

Gentleness creates family memories. Diffuses anger. Helps develop a healthy, loving family. Even in difficult conversations, or the challenge of disciplining our children, our impact is enhanced by gentle resolve. We appreciate gentleness. We internalize it in all our thinking, perception, and emotions. Gentleness is a choice. It is a powerful choice.

Gentleness creates the environment for our growth as families. It is easy to see the difference between children who have been raised in a mean, stressful, emotionally distant home and a healthy home. Gentle parents are kind, patient, protective, and nurturing. Gentleness keeps childish secrets from collecting in dark closets.

My parents enjoyed Little House on the Prairie, Andy Griffith and the Waltons. The shows always taught a lesson. Looking back at family disagreements, we could have used more gentleness. Gentle families stay on top of situations. Gentle families have strength under control. I was born in 1942 into a poor East Tennessee family. Families became experts at having little but making the most of what they had. Our joy was not in things or possessions, but it was within us.

For most of us, family life rides on a bumpy road. Our children and grandchildren, so cute and so beautifully created demands around the clock care. We experience joy during parenting. Joy is ours in Christ. Joy is a rare experience in most families.

Joy brings a full cup of blessings, and we overflow with joy in glory to God. We and our families will become intentional about joy. Outward circumstances are not in control. God is. Joy is practiced on purpose. Joy is deliberate, calculated, and conscious.

"Always rejoicing." How? Fear not. Negative emotions are like a piece of paper flying in the winds. Do not be distracted. We are children of God. Don't over-react. Choose gentleness and joy. The symbol of the Holy Spirit is a dove. The symbol for disciples of Christ is sheep, not a wolf.

The Word of God is showing us the way. Joy and gentleness go together. Joy embraces the coming of the Lord. The Lord is near. Embrace gentleness. Embrace joy. Self-serving people will never know the refreshing breeze of the joy and gentleness of Jesus. Sometimes the strongest Christian is running on empty. We lose sight of the one who shares love and is always behind us.

The parents of a young boy wanted to teach him responsibility. They required him to phone home when he arrived at a friend's house a few blocks away. Soon the son began to forget. He was confident that he could get home safely.

The first time he forgot, his dad called to be sure he had arrived. The son was told the next time it happened, he would have to come home. After a few days, the phone laid silent. The son was to know the consequences. His father dialed and prayed for wisdom. The telephone rang one time. A few seconds later, the phone rang again. It was the son. He said, "I'm here dad." The father asked, "What took you so long?"

The boy replied, 'Well Dad, we started playing. I just forgot. I heard the phone ring once, and I remembered."

With fatherly gentleness, he said, "I am sure glad you remembered. Have a fun time."

God is near to the brokenhearted. God saves those who are crushed in spirit. Live with the awareness and a connection to the presence of Jesus. You shall become gentle toward all people, regardless how they have treated you.

Teach children about the strength of gentleness. Be a strong hand with a gentle touch. Guard your tone of voice. When my daughter was a little girl, she would squeeze my hand as hard as she could. She thought she could make it hurt. She had no need to be gentle, because she lacked the power to cause me any pain.

Talk about how important gentleness is. Ask how it feels when a sibling or playmate is not gentle. Discuss other times when we practice being gentle.

My grandson is known as a gentle person. His mom taught him that being gentle brings awareness of strength. She helped him realize that gentleness is an attractive character trait. I admired her steady approach. It takes strength inside to be gentle on the outside.

Not everyone in the family has the ability to be gentle all the time. Some family members think that being gentle is a weakness. Their fear of showing gentleness is that somebody will take advantage of them. Couples who treat each other harshly and insensitively do not last.

Gentle family members smile often. The smiles encourage others to be comfortable with you. Smiles lighten the atmosphere for joy in family relationships. Smile often.

We can make suggestions, but we cannot force our will on anybody else. Respect the free will of everyone. Listen willfully. When your family member pours out sentiments, don't try to silence them.

During the pandemic, our family rarely drove to a grocery store. On the day, we first shopped, the aisles were crowded. Shelves were picked over. Prices were higher. We circled back to the cold food to pick up some bagels.

Other families were trying to get their food. I saw a young mother yelling at her child. The daughter had wandered too far from her mom. The mom yelled inappropriately. Customers wanted to say or do something. They wanted to hold the child and tell her she was pretty. However, nobody desired to interfere. Nobody did.

The pandemic, politics, and daily stress has been hard on families. There is real uncertainty when the pain will end. Our children and grandchildren are going to be disrupted for many years.
It is easy to lose sight of what we can control. We can cultivate small moments of joy in each day. Family gentle joy is simple. Our children have an enormous

capacity for joy. Joy can be infectious. There are things we can do to add joy. Baking is what our grandchildren enjoy. A box of brownie mixes and cookie dough works.

Paint and draw. Whatever the family uses to create pictures is perfect. Read out loud. Joy always results as we read to our children. Start with children's books. Our family enjoys the *Chronicles of Narnia*. Take turns reading if you have grown children. Play board games. Make up your own family board game. Build things from blocks, Legos, or cardboard. Build a fort. Build a city. Go for family walks. Put on music. Clear space and have fun.

Getting children to contribute to household chores benefits the whole family. There are many things we can do to increase our joy. There is joy in every moment if we would just look. Slowing down and being gentle create opportunities for joy.

If my readers want to find ways to have more joy with the children, watch grandparents. Most celebrate joy with their grandchildren far better than parents do. My wife and I enjoy spending time with our children and their families. Relationships are the center of our love and joy. Our joy cups are filled overflowing. Spending time with people we love is a sure-fire way to increase joy.

Touch, squeeze, hug. Long hugs are better than short hugs. Spend time in nature. We can talk and connect. As a family, find people to serve. Our family gives to needy families at Christmas and other occasions. We cook meals for people who are struggling. Be gentle. Slow down. Sit quietly. Play. Play brings communication. We listen. Build relationships. Laugh.

Remember the joy of watching your child gently sleep. Take time to look at your family photos. See old home movies. We are afraid of missing out. We overschedule. We deplete our family joy. Temporary happiness is not our goal. Happiness does not depend on what we have or what we do. A life of joy means that we know how to be gentle and loving no matter what.

That deep well of joy comes as a gift from God. Connection to Jesus requires space and time. Allow and encourage Bible reading, prayer, worship and other spiritual practices. Creating a joy-filled atmosphere may seem superficial. The home plays a vital role in the joy we and our family feel deep in their souls. Well-selected music playing in the background improves our moods. Activities and achievements are important. That is how children find their unique gifts.

There will be gentleness in the family that will influence the next generations for 10,000 years. Wow! Search your family roots. Find their life stories, their joys, their unique gifts. God has been loving your family from the first person to today.

A Gentle Conversation with God

O my minister of joy to the world. Learn everything you can to understand My ways. Take joy in using the new and the old to serve Me and to overcome the world.

Ministry depends on you and how you handle what is important. Remember, the wise servant used what he had in such a way that his original gifts multiplied.

With My wisdom, your ministry will continue to be effective. Never hide what I have given to you. Share them. I shall fill you with overflowing.

There are no bad apple ministers, ordained or lay in my fruit barrel. My Spirit produces good fruit. Stir up the ingredients. Fan the flame of your service. Stir up what is in you.

I call you to be My servant, not somebody to be admired. You are human, but I expect more of you. In the everyday working and walking, you will become what you are created to be. I knew you before your birth. I was in your family's presence in every family in your history.

Gentleness in the Humility

Humility is another underrated quality. It is important for growth. Being humble helps build trust. My definition of humility is an attitude that we have no special importance. Gentle people do not lack healthy pride. Humility is a type of modesty. Arrogant people are not humble. The best people in the world make mistakes. Those who cannot know their own weaknesses will never reach their full potential. Humble people take pride in their accomplishments. They sincerely want the best for others rather than try to hoard all the success. They apologize when they make a blunder.

In a culture of rough individualism, gentleness is thought of as a weakness, being soft and spineless. Biblical gentleness is strength under control. Gentleness is like a wild horse that has become obedient to a bit and bridle. It was not lack of power, but tremendous power under control. Gentleness means to find a loving way to do a job.

My wife served as the director of nursing of a dialysis center for more than 20 years. She had the tough task of hiring and firing nurses. When an employee performed poorly, she had to terminate them. She used tact, diplomacy, and gentleness.

The Bible teaches that gentleness is love's humility. It is strength under control. Matthew 11:29-30. Jesus tells us to take his yoke upon us and we will discover rest for our souls. That means to stop letting our own strength expressed through our fallen nature and giving over control to God.

Humility comes from the root word "humus" or earth. Humility is a reminder that we are the same. It is a key path to joy. It frees us to be real and to be connected with others. Humility is not something we claim for ourselves. Practicing humility enable our memory that when we are successful, we do not confuse our roles.

Insecurity is the biggest obstacle to humility. Advertisement messages depict the ways we are not enough. We attempt to be perfectionistic. We spend huge amounts of time and energy to project the image of being in control. We are enough.

We are the gifts of God. We are beloved children of God. None of us result from a divine accident. We are essential in God's eyes. Accept that truth and we are just us. We need not be someone we're not to cover up for God loves us just the way we are. We permit the light of God to shine through us. Humble people are never threatened by the gifts of others. Stretching beyond our comfort zones or embarrassing ourselves for our failures. Humility opens doors to gentleness to us and others. With that door wide open we admit when we are wrong. We praise others and give compliments. We apologize with sincerity or condition. We choose to go last at the traffic stop, in the grocery line, or any other place. We listen more than we talk.

Loving strong people make as many mistakes as weak people. The difference is that strong people admit them and learn from them. Our burden is light because Jesus has shown us the way. "The joy of the Lord" gives us strength to make the journey. (Calvin Miller, *Gentleness: Cultivating Spirit-Given Character*, pp. 1-11)

When Muhammad Ali was in his prime as a boxer, he boarded for an airplane flight. The stewardess reminded him to fasten his seat belt. Brashly he said, "Superman don't need no seat belt." The stewardess quickly said, "Superman don't need no airplane, either." Ali calmly fastened his belt. (James S. Hewett, *Illustrations Unlimited*, p. 295.

Love's humility acknowledges that we don't know what to do. We keep our lips shut. We silence our minds. We interrupt our defensive mind gab by not interfering. We accept everything as it happens with grace. We offer our humility through empathy. We recognize areas that need work. We are then open for improvement. That is where emotional intelligence is our oil to keep us going.

Our parents gave us life. Search in your life roots to find the names of the ancestors who had to live and survive, so we could exist. They lived at differing times. They braved unimaginable hardships. They faced injustice. They lived without things we take for granted, so that we could have the life we enjoy today.

We experience enormous joy and appreciation that comes with being in touch the many gifts that have been given.

Allowing ourselves to be vulnerable requires emotional courage. Treating ourselves gently is a sign of love. Being gentle to ourselves and embracing ourselves is crucial to success in building meaningful relationships. Humility the source for inner well-being. We can pick ourselves up after a downfall. Humble ones admit and recognize their part in the disaster. They work toward changing themselves.

Being gentle with babies is easy and natural. Babies love hearing a gentle voice. They love feeling a gentle touch. Babies feel secure and deeply loved in a safe atmosphere.

Creating such emotional and physical safety is a process. Feeling safe allows our gentle nature to surface and to be expressed. Growing up, we lose touch with the concept of being gentle. Exposing ourselves to an emotionally toxic environment creates long lasting negative impacts on our well-being.

As a therapist and as a pastor, I see an emotional shutdown, defensiveness, and reactivity as the coping strategies to deal with the toxicities. The joy we feel has little to with the realities and circumstances, and everything to do with the focus of our lives. It has been my experience that gentleness includes humility, forgiveness, and kindness. Empathetic folks have high social intelligence, a deep tenderness in loving others. They are gentle in their curious questioning.

Humble people have a quiet ego. They are quick to let things go and to forgive. They demonstrate kindness with a soft and supportive demeanor. Gentle souls walk softly from place to place. They humbly attend to people they encounter.

In this world gentleness matters. Perhaps some of our new scientists will do more research. Researchers can study strengths together. Therapists and medical practitioners can bring gentleness in approaching their clients.

Life would have more love and joy if we would be gentle with ourselves, our families, our colleagues, even those who fail or disappoint us. Failures create inferior and false impressions of ourselves. We need to build our confidence. Humility helps us recognize our strengths. Success is a series of small wins. These motivate to be better and to burst out of our comfort zones. If we are comfortable about being uncomfortable, we become unstoppable. Writing goals in a journal and read them often. Keeping a positive mindset helps us gain and maintain humility. Reminding ourselves of our talents will continue our improvement.

Some folks define gentleness as restraining of power. They believe that gentleness requires the strong to withdraw their power. I do not think this is the nature of being gentle. Gentleness is best seen by looking at the object, not the subject. It is about the Golden Rule or how another is being treated, whether we are stronger than them or weaker. Treating someone gently is not asserting ourselves above them. Gentleness is a form of love.

Being gentle has its risks. Perhaps the reader remembers J.R.R. Tolkein's *Return of the King*. Denethor speaks with the noble Faramir. He says, "Ever your desire is to appear lordly and generous as a king of old, gracious, gentle. That may well fit one of high race, if he sits in power and peace. But in desperate hours gentleness may be paid with death."

"So be it," replied Faramir.

That is the risk. Gentleness is not always repaid in kind. For us to act gently, we need the assurance that the risk is worth it. Faramir acknowledges that gentleness is the right way to be and act, regardless of the circumstances. Faramir believes it is truth. A bigger truth suggests to him that gentleness is best. We are graced.

A Gentle Conversation with God

With your humility, I shall hear you praise Me. Your attitude of praise reaches out and touches all My people. Those who live in My humility will find My joy as their strength when they become discouraged. When I know you and love you more and more each day, it is like giving Me a bucket of cool water on a hot day.

My Word is an active love of your soul. I will accompany you on your life journey. Clanging voices and distractions will demand your attention. If you will follow te inner light, you will get more insight into My Kingdom overflowing like a beautiful flower. My light shines on you, Do I need to say more?

Gentleness in the Strongest Power

In 70 years of pastoral ministry, I have conducted hundreds of weddings. One incredible and memorable was with a huge defensive lineman from the University of Nebraska Cornhuskers. He stood quietly at the church altar with his petite bride. They recited their marriage vows and added, "I will always be gentle with you."

The wedding inspired my understanding of how Christians should be gentle on every occasion. I have heard few sermons on gentleness. The apostle Paul listed gentleness in eighth place on the list of essential fruit of the Spirit.

Gentleness is not a weak or fragile thing. Gentle people find strength in their identity as being created in the image of God. They nurture their spiritual lives by encountering Jesus Christ. Their souls are transformed from being weak and sin-sick to being strong and healthy.

Strong women and men are tempted to act as bullies. The biblical call is to find God's holiness which lies in the souls of those who live in Christ. Martin Buber said that we are dealing with the sacred Thou when we are with each other. Failure of strong people to be gentle is the foundation of our problems.

"Gentleness is not weakness. Just the opposite. Preserving a gentle spirit in a heartless world takes extraordinary courage, determination, and resilience.

Do not underestimate the power of gentleness, because gentleness is strength wrapped in peace, and therein lies the power to change the world," said L.R. Knost. Joy is based on being content regardless of circumstances. We can store in our videos of life memories of joy which builds our resources when times are difficult.

Strong people go softly, slowly, and sweetly. They will get down on one knee to listen to a child. They look at them in the eyes. Gentleness is shown in the lightness of a feather in the hand. Or a bird in hand. Observing nature and wildlife with an awe and reverence. They carefully walk on eggshells of a sensitive or difficult conversation. They handle adversity with calmness and a smile.

Gentleness is shown with an unwavering hand that knows how to walk a life's pathway. There is an inner silence at times of struggle or wonder. Selah! A teacher disciplines an out-of-control, rude student with gentleness without a raised voice or undue harshness. We treat the weak and broken with soft hands. It is easy to crush another person. Deeply damaged people operate from their place of hurting.

Human beings are complex. "A gentle voice turns away anger." Outrage brings on more outrage. Anger is frightening. Peace and restraint with gentle answers exposes anger. Risk being gentle.

In his book, *Of Mice and Men*, John Steinbeck inserts a giant of a man named Lennie. Lennie is as strong as an ox. He has big muscles and down deep a gentle heart. He has a mental disability. He is not aware of his own strength. He loves to pet soft things. Lennie unintentionally kills a mouse. He kills a puppy while he is stroking her. Finally, he accidently and fatally breaks a woman's neck.

Power in its many forms is a gift from God. Power is dangerous when used improperly. The answer to the problem is not its loss but gaining gentleness. Gentleness in our time is the single most misunderstood fruit of the Spirit. Gentleness is a positive spin on weakness. The biblical concept of gentleness is not a lack of strength. It is an exercise of divine power.

Consider rain. Hard rain destroys life, but gentle rain gives life. Violent rain does harm. Wise farmers do not pray for weak rain or no rain, but for gentle rain.

The apostle Peter contrasts good power with bad power. We desire strong leaders, not weak ones. Sheep are weak and vulnerable. They need a strong shepherd, not a weak one.

My strong daughter Linda has never wanted a weak daddy. She wants me to be strong. She needs me to flex my muscles over her. As a child, she realized that her daddy was bigger and stronger than her. She needed me to also to be gentle.

Weak men are preoccupied with talking and showing their strength. Strong men let their gentleness be known to all. They have demonstrated how to be a channel of God's gentleness. Their strength is under restraint and self-control. Paul says being gentle is never optional, but essential in leadership. Titus 3:1-2, II Timothy 2:24-25. Strong men, and strong women do everything, including their encounter with their opponents with gentleness.

Biblical gentleness is formed and filled by God. God is the gentle paragon. God is even more admirable because our Creator knows how to wield power in ways that give life rather than death to the beloved.

God is not like Lennie in Steinbeck's novel. Jesus descended gently into our world in Bethlehem. He grew in wisdom and stature in Nazareth. He taught with tenderness in Galilee. He rode into Jerusalem humble and mounted on an ordinary donkey. Jesus was powerful enough to become gentleness himself.

A Gentle Conversation with God

Gentleness is never a false modesty. It is not self-depreciation. It is not spineless. Be responsible with your power. My plan is surely the best one possible. Listen to Me. In each of our inner conversations, I will guide you. My power is the only one that matters.

Filled with Me, put on an apron and serve. Power erases any feeling of inferiority. Power comes with respect, a desire to benefit others, and genuine love.

I greatly enjoy being with you. I keep cherishing you when you are unable to do the things you want to do on your own. You really need Me. If we stay together, we will fill the world with powerful love.

Gentleness in the Lost and Found

Most people watched Superman movies and television shows. In his everyday life, he was the mild, gentle reporter Clark Kent. Kent showed gentleness. How can be find gentleness when we have lost it? Matthew 5:5. Living gently is impossible on our own. We recognize that it was impossible even for Superman.

When I served as a therapist for Lutheran Family Services, I experienced a moment that is stored in my life video. It was a cold winter day in north Omaha, Nebraska at 24th and Lake Streets. Night had not fallen. It was beginning to get dark. Therapists always walked out of the building with two or more people.

When we walked out, there was a woman in crisis. Her clothing hung off her bony frame. She was covered with sores. She was attempting to dance on the street. She was wildly distressed. I felt frozen. Another woman therapist remained calm. She approached her gently. She asked gingerly what was wrong. Her voice was soothing, but strong. The young woman was addicted to heroin. Her fear was clear. Her story was disjointed.

She asked us to call an ambulance to take her to the University of Nebraska Medical Center. My fellow therapist maintained her caring way. She lightly touched her. She kept listening carefully. She kept her eyes on her with tenderness. I so admired the therapist's demeanor. She had a gentle soul. Her gentle approach fortified a young person in crisis. Her gentleness nourished me. I saw the power to soothe and make a change. I deepened my commitment to gentleness. I wore it like a cloak, flowing softly and creating an aura of tenderness.

Gentleness is rare. We are born in sin. Its human nature as we have deep paths worn into us after years of walking according to our flesh. Our feet have become so used to slogging through harsh mire and muck when we are shackled with heavy burdens. Gentleness is rare. We continue to think and live like we did when we were not believers.

Scripture says sanctification is the process of growing out of our old behavior as we become mature believers. Gentleness creates the atmosphere for our maturity. It creates a soft surface for learning how to deal with the hard rocks of life. People fail to find gentleness. That's just not their nature. We must permit God's word to wash us, break us, convict us, renew us, heal us, Gentleness comes as our reactions change. We have found it as our fear, worry, and anger become a thing of the past. We become thankful for God's blessings. We sleep in peace because our conscience is clean. Relationships have been restored. The tone in our voice softens. Our eyebrows are not separated by a deep furrow. We smile more.

People around us notice and wonder what we have found. Unusual things happen. We attract new friends. People honor us with their lips. Our children begin to share their innermost thoughts. Strangers call upon us for counsel. People are drawn to us. Our spouses become our friends. Ministry opportunities begin to crop up in amazing places. Learning and living become a joyful experience when gentleness is the rule. Once we have found it, we never want to lose it again. (Elizabeth George, *Putting on a Gentle and Quiet Spirit*, pp. 165-180)

The sad truth is we often do not treat each other gently. Our cruelty to one another is commonplace. Think back to the school playground to remember the sheer ordinariness of meanness to each other.

As mature adults, we must practice gentleness. Recovering gentleness is not easy, especially in these ungentle times. Gentleness is against our cultural grain. No wonder there is so much domestic violence and abuse of the gift of sexuality. There are deeper divisions, more contempt, and more anxiety. Deep fear is the problem. Gentleness means being troubling. We desire it, but it has become inadmissible. If they are not despised, gentle ones are persecuted. We possess divided minds.

We have learned and accepted from childhood that this is a brutal world. One must become brutal to survive. Regrettably, some people try to forcefully push the Bible and their own view of religion on the world in an unloving manner. Uncompassionately, they rebuke people with Bible verses. Some even scorn their unrighteous behavior.

These methods cause division and for some to neve go to any church forever. As I shared the miracle of our lost and found group, "Lost people act like they are lost because they are lost.

Lost young people cannot act any other way than who they are. Even the most skilled and influential human persuasion is insufficient to save them from their sins. Most needy youth are attractive and sexy, but they are lost. People tell them how desired they are. They invite them to parties and introduce them to drugs that addict them into more destruction. They will die in their sins if they do not repent. We must gently share the gospel in love. Ephesians 4:15. We are to be faithful witnesses in giving personal testimonies of what Christ has done in our lives.

Jesus did not give us the role of condemning the lost. We are to speak the truth in love so the lost can choose to be released from their condemnation. John 3:16-18.

Christ did not call us to argue for the gospel as an attorney or judge might do. We tell what we have seen and heard firsthand.

Every believer has a personal testimony to share what Christ has done for them. We tell who we were before we came to Jesus, how we came to him, what Christ has done, and who we are in Christ.

If that is your genuine testimony, it is hard to challenge. People will argue over points of disagreement, but nobody can argue against your testimony, because you are the expert of your testimony.
Some in our youth group became newborns in Christ. I

had the privilege of baptizing many of them. They even grew to the point of testifying about their salvation and becoming a new person through Christ.

We are encountering those who are lost. They have been trapped and dead in their sin. Most, at first, will be resistant and skeptical. Keep on trying. Allow the Holy Spirit to work in the heart of the hearer. Rest in the power of the Word of God and the spirit of God to do their work.

Our responsibility lies in serving as witnesses, sharing the gospel with the lost, speaking God's work with compassion, love, and gentleness. We need to be faithful to the direction of the Holy Spirit. Romans 10:14.

A Gentle Conversation with God

Lost and Found was the name chosen by those in the youth group at First Christian Church in Weeping Water. I was there and I approved your ministry to hose needy and confused youth.

None of these young people wanted to expose their faults. Thank you for keeping everything confidential. I sent My Spirit of love into every one of them. I know you felt the agony of their wrong choices and never giving up on them.

I clearly knew the congregation had been divided and weak. Their selfish attitudes destroyed the unity they could have enjoyed.

I never give up on my chosen ones. Let the old pass away. Walk in the newness with Me. I am ready at any moment to forgive those who turn around, determined to leave behind their old ways that left Me out.

Gentleness in the Joy

One reason I decided to write this book was to help me and others to be gentler. When I am gentle, I feel so loved and people are easier to get along with. Just writing about gentleness has given me a deeper sense of joy.

Serving as the Minister of Joy to the World, how could I not connect gentleness with joy. Join me in this exciting journey to seek an understanding of joy and gentleness and how they are related.

When we do actions with gentleness, we get a wonderful feeling inside. Psalm 37:3. Saying and writing gentle words is a sure way to experience joy. What gentleness is, how to be gentle, and the emotional benefits of gentleness are in this book.

Perhaps my readers have specific people in their lives toward whom you want to be gentler. Some want to be more gentle in general to those you encounter in the life journey, and have trouble being consistent, then these words will not be written in vain. I am an emotionally sensitive introvert. That has been a benefit, especially when trying to understand others. It has made me a better pastor, an effective therapist, teacher, and writer. Being emotionally sensitive has also given me pain. I speak with authority on a topic such as gentleness.

That is why I have enjoyed my ministry so much. I have had a joy impacting opportunity to be gentle to people in desperate circumstances. Despite knowing the joy that gentleness brings, I am not always gentle.

The dark side of me is impatient, too easily frustrated, and not always shining my light of joy on friends, colleagues, family members, and those with whom I communicate.

Paul uses the term "standing firm." The apostle means steadily resisting the negative influences of temptation, false teaching, and persecution. To stand firm requires endurance when we are opposed or challenged.

Gentleness is joy outward expressed. The Greek word for gentleness is a difficult word to fully translate into English. It refers to a spirit that is reasonable, fair-minded, and generous. It means we are willing to give up our own rights to show consideration to others. William Barclay said, "There is no virtue in the Christian life which is not made radiant with joy. There is no circumstance and no occasion which is not illuminated by joy. A joyless life is not a Christian life, for joy is one constant recipe for Christian living." (James Hewett, op. cit., p. 15)

Every moment of life cannot be filled with joy. We appreciate joy because joy comes in a surprise. We cannot create it. Gentleness and joy have added to my mental fortitude. As I look forward, these are two fruits of the Spirit that I shall keep close throughout my life and share with the needy world. Helen Keller noted, "Joy is the holy fire that keeps our purpose warm and our intelligence aglow." (Ibid., p. 11)

Gentleness has resonated with me, along with joy. Both reflect how I want to live my life. Gentleness and joy complement each other quite well. I attempt to be calm and even tempered. I seek healthy avenues of joy. I remind myself to maintain a rounded perspective and a balanced mind. This is not easy for me. All my life I have been rather quiet and reserved. Society expects us to socialize more. I am never afraid to be alone. How else could I produce so many books, preach so many sermons, and express myself. I never liked the typical college life. I have been near exhaustion trying to cope. I recognize who I am as being gentle and experiencing joy. I hold myself to high ethics and personal values.

I ask for advice and direction. I listen closely and my opinions can change. Gentleness means listening, setting an example, and recognizing moral flaw. These are missing in our political structure. Immoral actions go unchecked and then unchecked again and again. I am aware that many politicians break the rules but get a pass. I have had confidence in who I am and the thoughtful choices and risks I have taken. I have been intrinsically motivated. The idea of valuing my choices is where joy, or the lack of it, enter my life picture. I have let my guard down. I have trusted those who were proven that cannot be trusted.

I have not valued my time or my accomplishments, which kills joy. Spending an hour conducting worship in a nursing home or jail is not an hour lost. Time helping a friend is not time lost. Activities such as writing alone does not mean I am lonely. When we become known for our gentleness, we become our best advocate. We agree with God as joy and gentleness are interpedently related. Joy comes from within. We rejoice in the Lord. We hold on to praise not anger.

Gentleness, joy, and peace are a cord of three strands. They work for those who work for righteousness. They work for those who are peacemakers. That unity is tight and is not easily undone.

Gentleness ripples outward. If we cannot be gentle with ourselves, we cannot be gentle with others. Gentleness starts from within. When gentleness starts from within, it echoes out. It impacts other people's lives. We all experience the love and grace of God together. Love operates magnificently, abounding by the grace of God into other lives.

The biggest mistake we can make is not being gentle enough with ourselves. We are too quick to condemn. God who is in love with us will soothe our souls. Mother Teresa said, "A joyful heart is the normal result of a heart burning with love. She gives most who gives with joy."

The apostle Paul expects gentleness to be produced from joy. Gentleness is the best one-word translation for the Greek word Paul used. We lose our sense of gentleness when we forget that we are God's children. We are royalty in the family of God. We are safe and secure in divine protection.

Joy makes a difference. It is not false peppiness. It is not a false smile. Joy replaces guilt. The joy of Jesus' resurrection gives us eternal life. We are not spiritual survivors rescued from disaster. We now belong to heaven.

We act with gentle joy. We live with the Holy Spirit inside that gives believers a common hope. God writes our names in the "Book of Life." We share a common purpose. We share a common sense in each step of our development. We cherish the patience of other people.

Unresolved conflict thrives with a horizontal view of life. Continuing conflict exalts self-interest, promote prejudice, and drains away human joy. Gentle joy pursues a vertical view of life. Gentle joy is willing to "agree with each other in the Lord." We refuse to be imprisoned by conflict. With gentle joy, every child of God will design and produce "unity in the spirit." Ephesians 4:3

All creatures want to live a pleasure-filled life for the brief moments we exist on the earth. Fortunately, we do not need intelligence to experience joy. (Justin Gregg, *If Nietzsche Were a Narwhal*, p. 209)

We can squeeze joy out of togetherness. Joy causes us to rely on each other to build an atmosphere for joy. (Ross Gay, *Inciting Joy*, p. 17)

A Gentle Conversation with God

Jim, I have shown you that the joy of Mine is your strength. As you move out in My love to those who need Me, I shall fill you more and more to the brim. You will overflow with the sureness of My presence. Expect that My ways will make a difference.

Delight in Me. Calming delight, cheerful gladness will be in My dwelling place. My joy in you will seek those who are condemned by the world as hopeless.

My gift of joy is tender, kind, patient. Rejoice with Me as I find my lost sheep.

My vision always is imagined as too complex. Read the stories recorded in My Word. I promise you will get insights into things you have never seen before.

Bibliography

Barclay, William. *The Letters to the Corinthians.* Philadelphia: Westminster Press, 1958.

Barclay, William. T*he Letters of the Galatians and Ephesians.* Philadelphia: Westminster Press, 1958.

Bauer, Arndt and Danker Gingrich. *A Greek Lexicon of the New Testament and Other Early Christian Literature.* Chicago: University of Chicago Press, 1979.

Bennett, William J. *The Book of Virtues.* New York: Simon & Schuster, 1993.

Dufourmantelle, Anne. Translated by Katherine Payne and Vincent Salle. *Power of Gentleness: Meditations on the Risk of Living.* New York: Fordham University Press, 2018.

Eyre, Jacalyn. *Gentleness: The Strength of Being Tender.* Grand Rapids, Michigan: Zondervan, 2001.

Gay, Ross. *Inciting Joy.* New York: Algonquin Publishers, 2022.

Gendler, J. Ruth. *The Book of Qualities.* Berkley, California: Turquoise Mountain Publications, 1984.

George, Elizabeth. *Putting On a Gentle and Quiet Spirit.* Eugene, Oregon: Harvest House Publishers, 2012.

Gregg, Justin. *If Nietzsche Were a Narwhal.* New York:

Little and Brown Publishers, 2022.

Hewett, James S. *Illustrations Unlimited*, Wheaton, Illinois: Tyndale House Publishers, 1988.

Horton, Stanley M. *What the Bible Says About the Holy Spirit.* Springfield, Missouri: Gospel Publishing House, 1976.

Killinger, John R. *Outgrowing Church.* Eugene, Oregon: Wipl & Stock Press, 2019.

Killinger, John R. *Prayer: The Act of Being with God.* Waco, Texas: Word Books Publisher, 1981.

King, Maxwell. *Good Neighbor: The Life and Work of Fred Rogers.* New York: Harry E. Abrams Publishers, 2018.

Larson, Craig Brian and Brian Lowery. *1001 Quotations That Connect: Timeless Wisdom for Preaching, Teaching, and Writing.* Grand Rapids, Michigan: Zondervan Publishing House, 2009.

Leadership Ministries Worldwide. *Practical Illustrations: Galatians, Ephesians, Philippians, Colossians.* Chattanooga, Tennessee: Leadership Ministries Worldwide Publishers, 2002.

MacIntyre, Alasdair. *After Virtue: A Study in Moral Theory.* Notre Dame, Indiana: University of Notre Dame Press, 1981.

McReynolds, James E. *Dancing with God: A Theology of Joy.* Cleveland, Tennessee: Parson's Porch Books, 2016.

McReynolds, James E. *Joy Comes in the Mourning: Love Is Forever.* Cleveland, Tennessee: Parson's Porch Books, 2020.

McReynolds, James E. *Spirit of Joy Church.* Cleveland, Tennessee: Parson's Porch Books, 2019.

McReynolds, James E. The *Joy of Prayer: The Way to Intimacy with God.* Cleveland, Tennessee: Parson's Porch Books, 2020.

McReynolds, James E. *The Joy of the Kingdom; Envisioning the Great Commission.* Cleveland, Tennessee: Parson's Porch Books, 2020.

McReynolds, James E. *The Spirituality of Joy: The Least Discussed Human Emotion.* Cleveland, Tennessee: Parson's Porch Books, 2011.

Miller, Calvin. *Gentleness: Cultivating Spirit-Given Character.*
Nashville: Thomas Nelson Incorporated, 2000.

Ortlund, Dane C. *Gentle and Lowly: The Heart of Christ for Sinners and Sufferers.* New York: Crossway, 2020.

Pearse, Mark Guy. *The Gentleness of Jesus.* New York: Creative Media Partners, 2018.

Peterson, Christopher and Martin E. P. Seligman. *Character Strengths and Virtues: A Handbook and Classification.* Oxford, England: Oxford University Press, 2004.

Reynolds, William J. *Joyful Sound*. New York: Holt, Rinehart, and Winston, 1978.

Sanders, Ella Francis. *Everything Beautiful: A Guide to Finding Hidden Beauty in the World.* New York: Penguin Life Publishing House, 2022.

Simpson, James. *Ordained to Ministry: Every Christian's Purpose for Being.* Cleveland, Tennessee: Pentecostal Institute of Church Growth, 1989.

Skinner, Torpy. "Navigating Changes," p. 31, *The Upper Room*, Nashville: Methodist Publishing House, September-October 2022.

Stramn, Raymond T. "Galatians, Exegesis," *The Interpreters Bible.* New York: Abingdon Press, 1953.

Wicks, Robert J. *Living a Gentle and Passionate Life.* New York: Paulist Press, 2020.

Wood, D. R. W. and Howard, Marshall. *New Bible Dictionary.* Leicester, England: Inner/Varsity Press, 1996.

Willard, Dallas. *The Allure of Gentleness: Defending the Faith in the Manner of Jesus.* San Francisco: Harper and Sons, 2016.

Wuthnow, S.D. *Sharing the Journey: Support Groups and America's New Quest for Community.* New York: Free Press, 1994.

Zinnbauer, B. J. "Spiritual Conversion: A Study of Religious Change Among College Students," *Journal for the Scientific Study of Religion*, 37, 165-180, 1998.

Notes About the Author

Dr. James E. McReynolds shares Visionquests for Joy throughout the world. "Your preaching embraced with joy, will be, as my positive thinking, a fresh vision for communicating Christian faith. Jim, I anoint you minister of joy to the world," Dr. Norman Vincent Peale declared during a School for Practical Christianity in New York.

His ministry has revolutionized the lives of countless people. Jim's calling has included preaching, teaching, writing, radio and television, psychotherapy, blogs, prayer, and innovative ways to share the joy that he has gently shared.

He served on the state board of directors of the Mental Health Association in Nebraska. He is a diplomat of the World Pastor Care Center, the pastoral care committee of the Baptist World Alliance, founding member of the American Association of Counselors, member of the International Positive Psychology Association, member of the prayer and spiritual formation task force of the Cooperative Baptist Fellowship, member and consultant for the Radio-Television Commission of the Southern Baptist Convention, the United Methodist Mental Health Network, and the Presbyterian Mental Health Network, and associate member of the American Association of Marriage and Family Therapy.

The author served as a public relations specialist with the Sunday School Board of the Southern Baptist

Convention and the Department of Mental Health in Missouri. He is a retired licensed mental health practitioner in Tennessee and Nebraska.

The governor of Nebraska named him an admiral in the Great Navy of the State of Nebraska, with an honorary certificate for his life work.

The Holston Conference of the United Methodist Church awarded his churches 20 gold, silver, and bronze certificates for excellence in evangelism. The Christian Church (Disciples of Christ) in the United States and Canada presented six excellences in evangelism awards.

The Christian Church (Disciples of Christ) in Nebraska honored him with a plaque that read: "Minister of Joy to the World for his faithful and dedicated service, 2010-2015. We thank him for his high-quality leadership as the regional moderator."

McReynolds also served as the regional representative for Global Missions of the Christian Church (Disciples of Christ) and the United Church of Christ. His world travels to share as minister of joy to the world were acknowledged by the World Missionary Distinction Award by the Council for World Mission in London.

Contact James McReynolds at 320 North Fourth Street, Elmwood, NE 68349. Email him at joyminister@windstream.net. His website is jamesevansmcreynolds.com. His phone number is 402-994-2370.

www.ingramcontent.com/pod-product-compliance
Lightning Source LLC
Chambersburg PA
CBHW060440090426
42733CB00011B/2348